AF573860

fluss flux flow fluency current stream river

In memory of my mother Stephania Magdalena

MICHAEL LANGE fluss

HATJE
CANTZ

you me when I think really think about it
are the same

Ikkyû

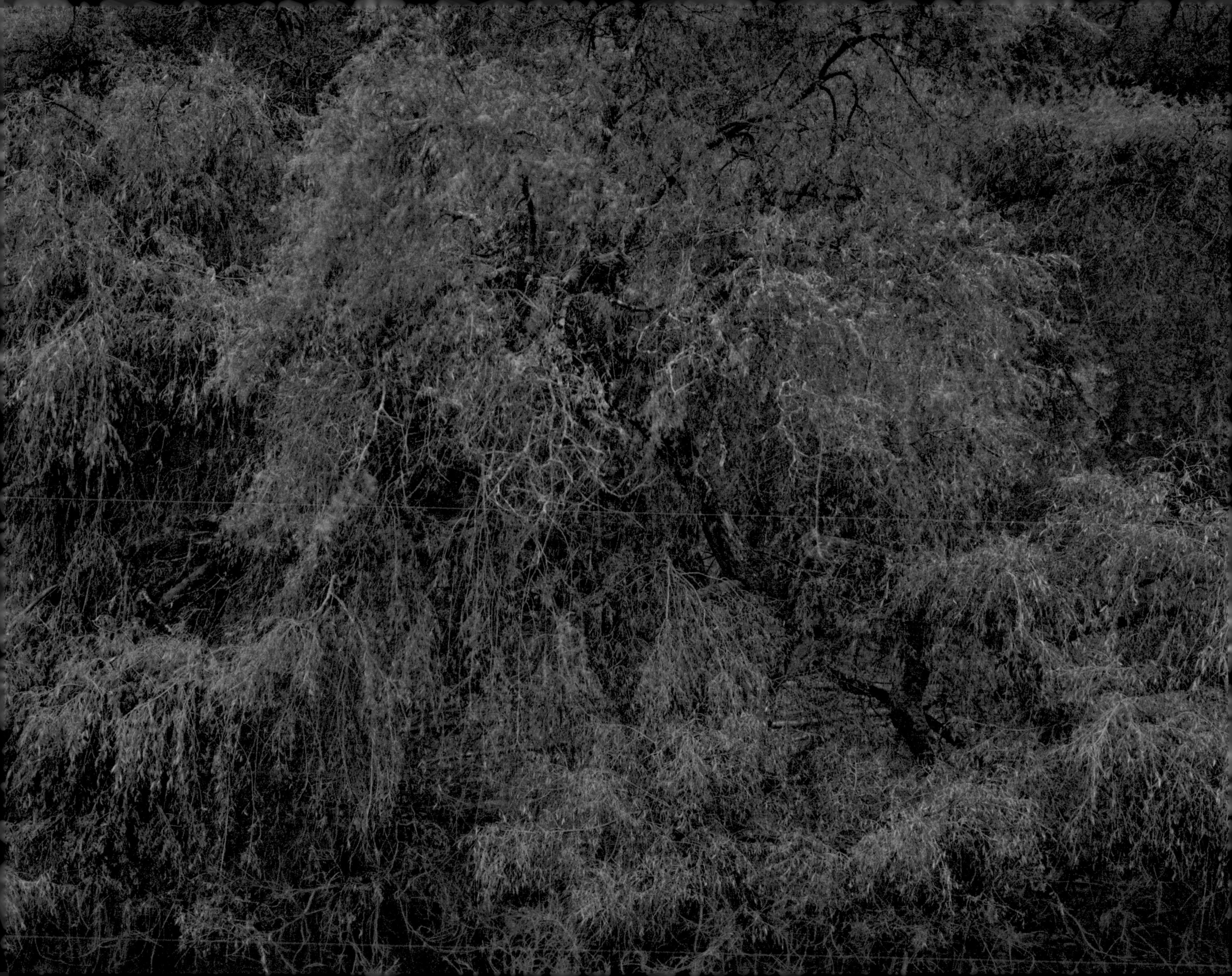

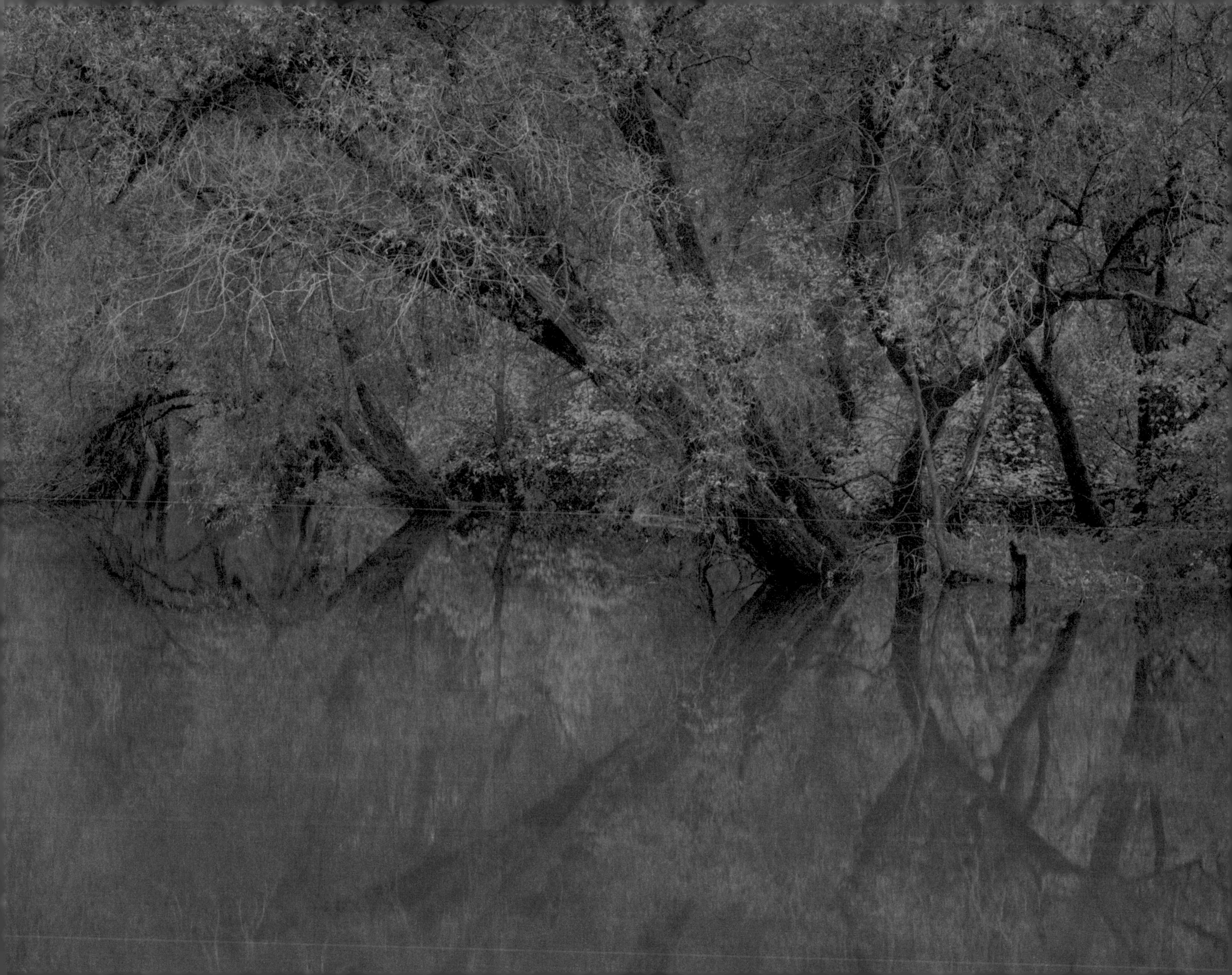

R 1924

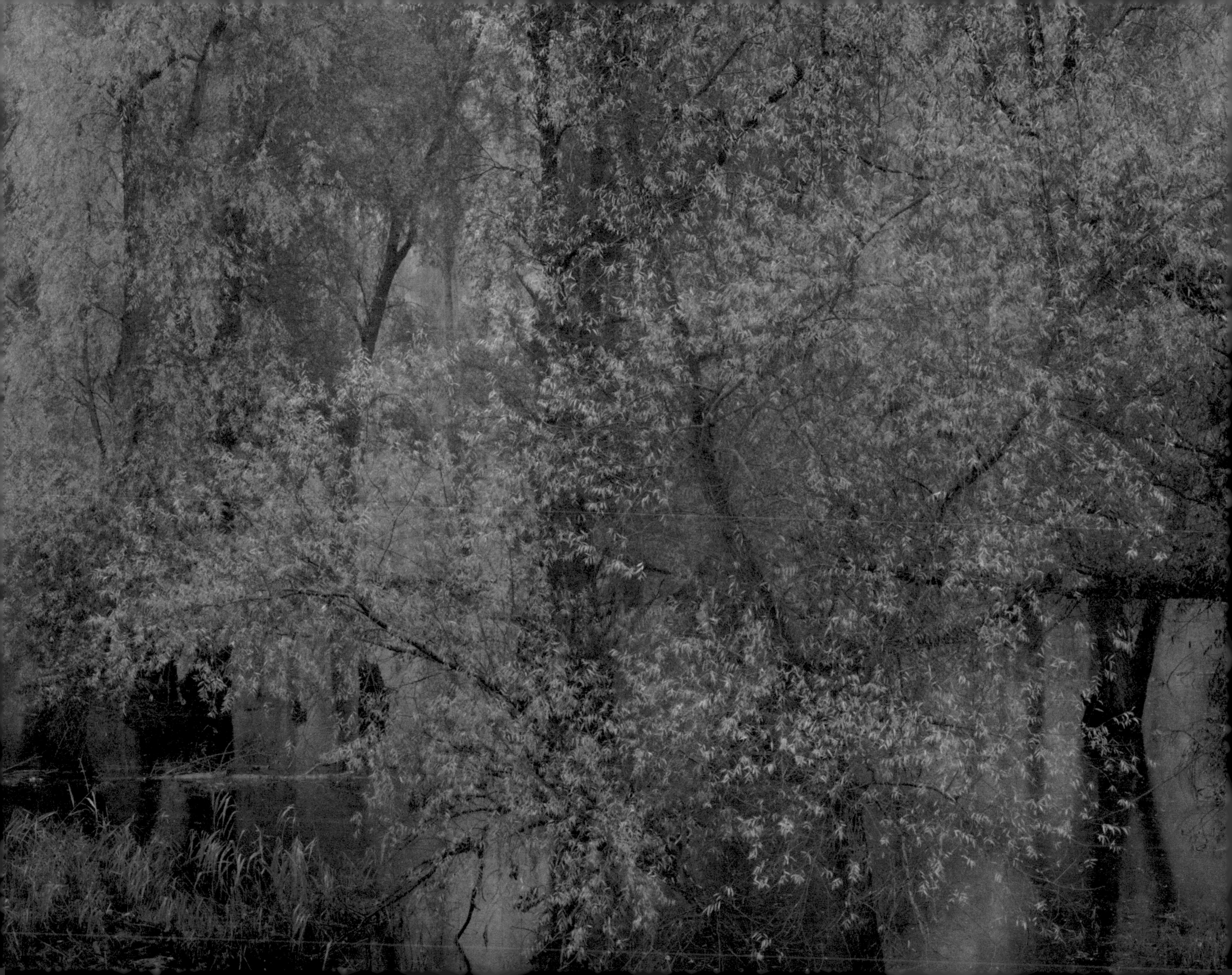

R 2808

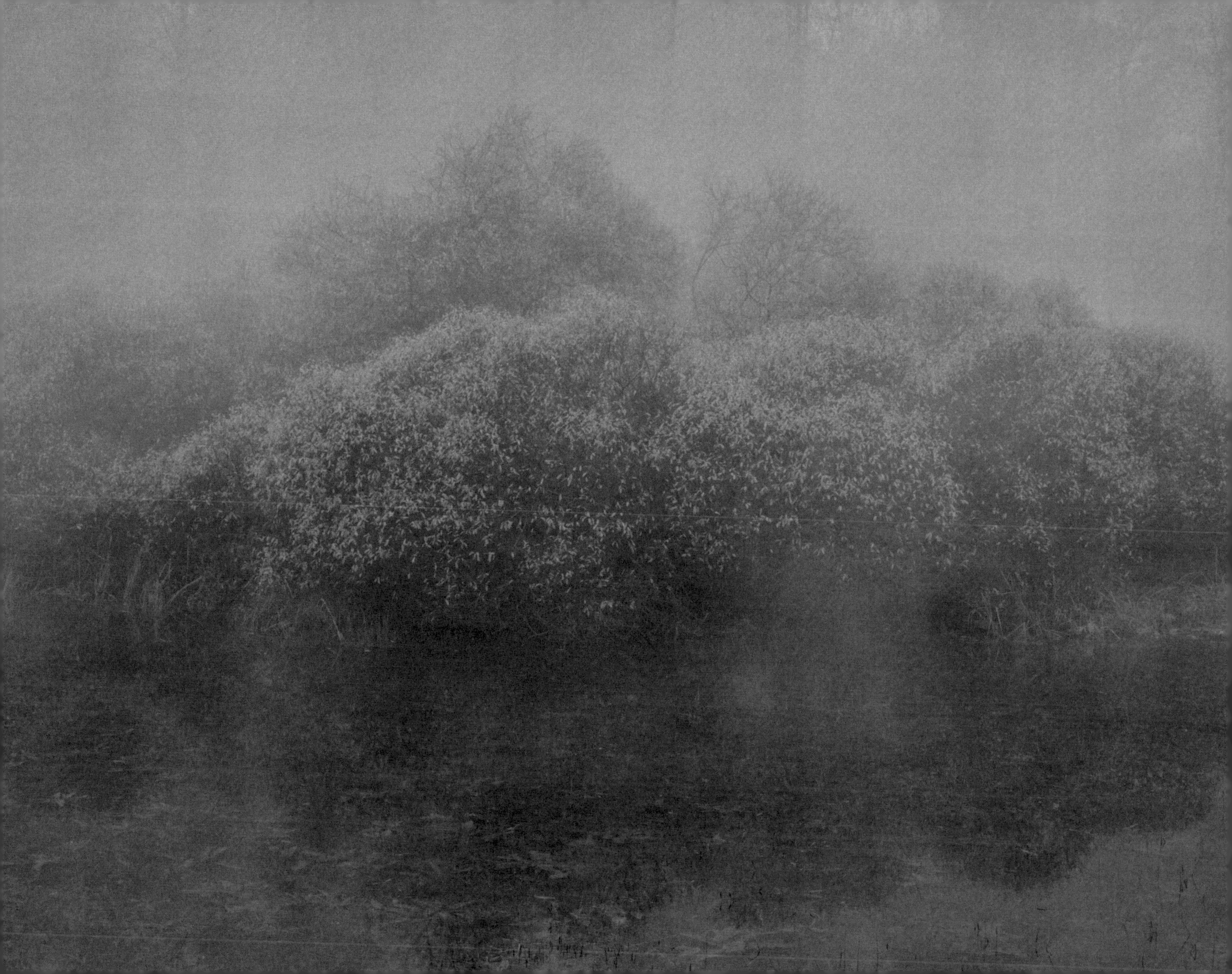

R 7720

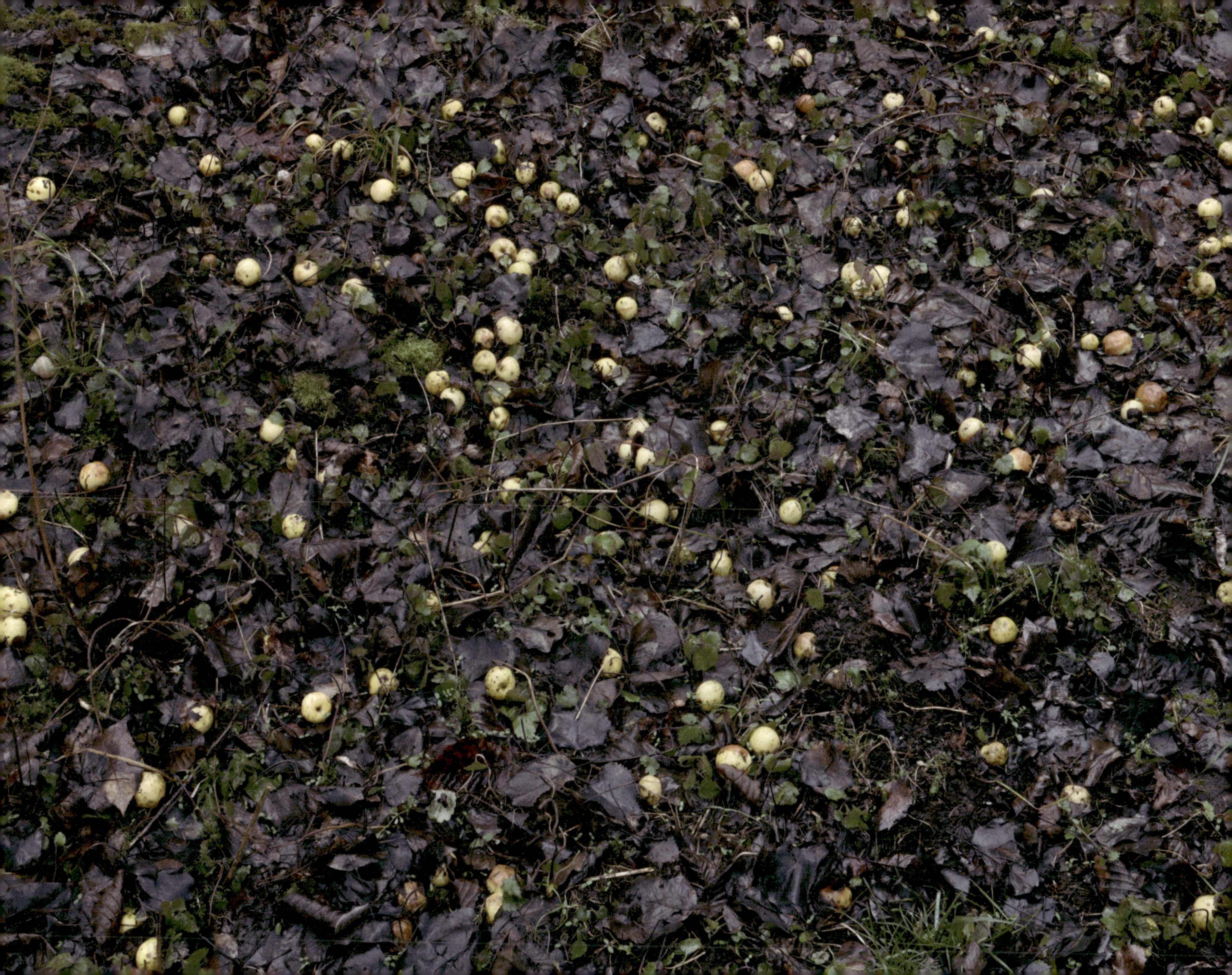

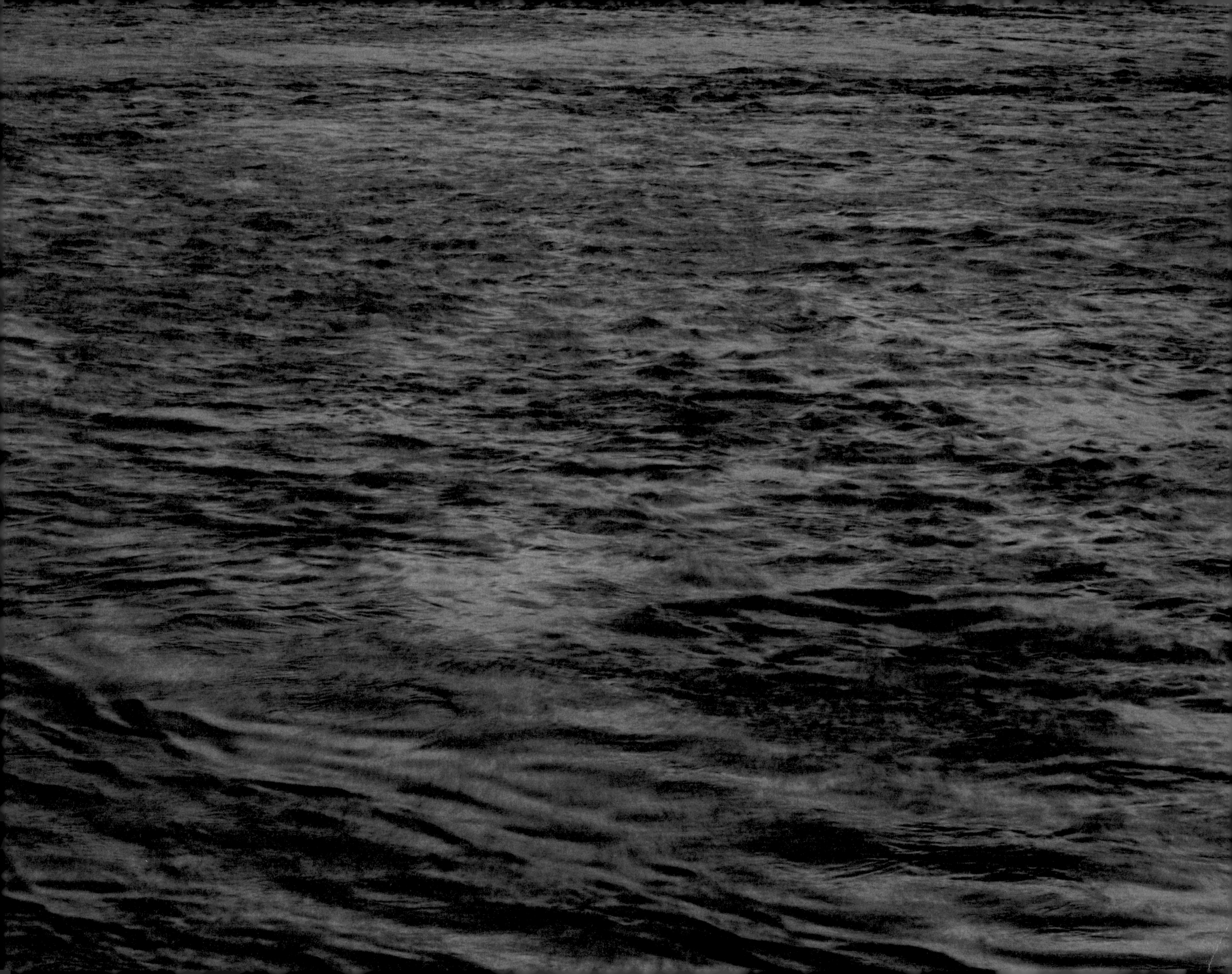

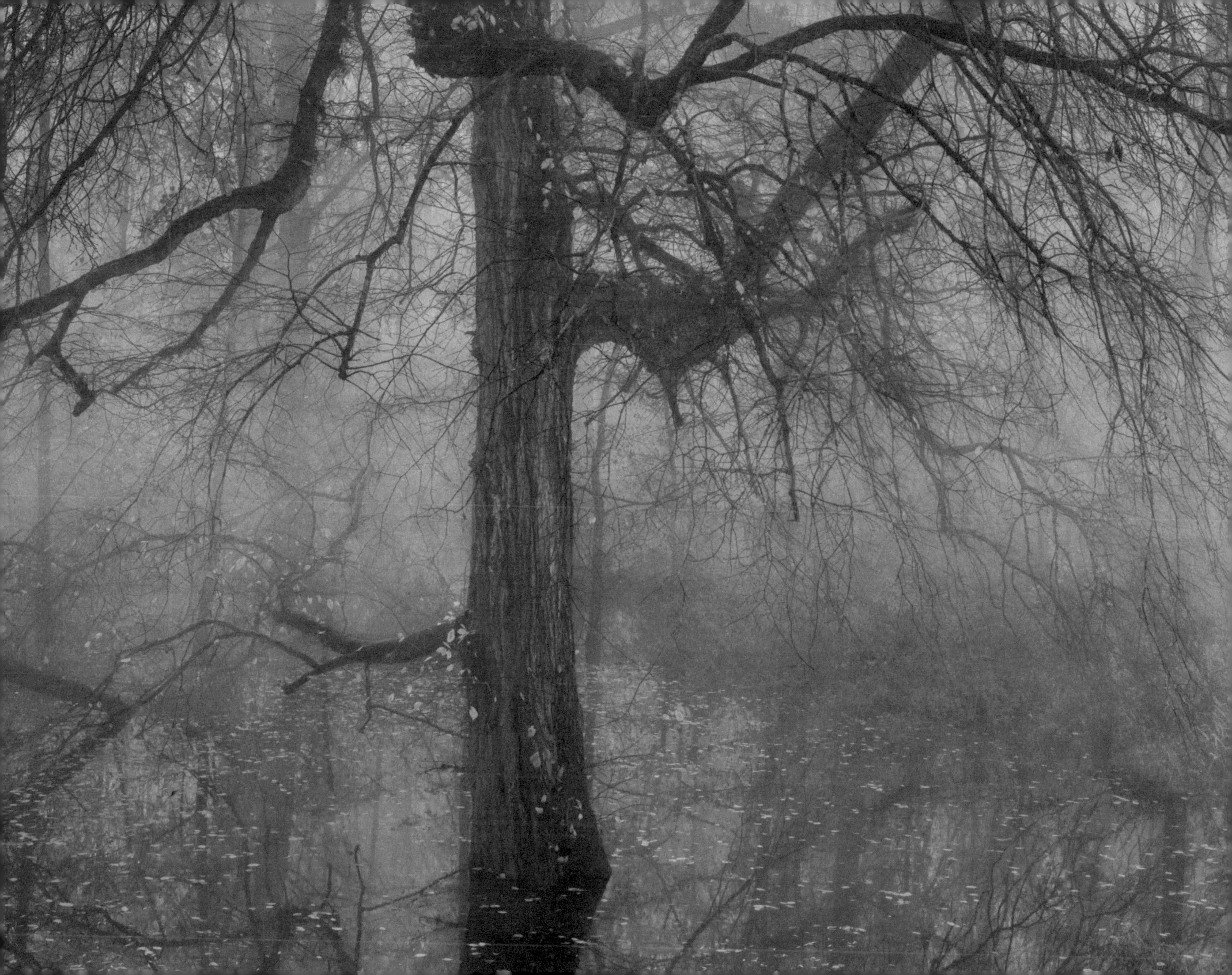

R 10217

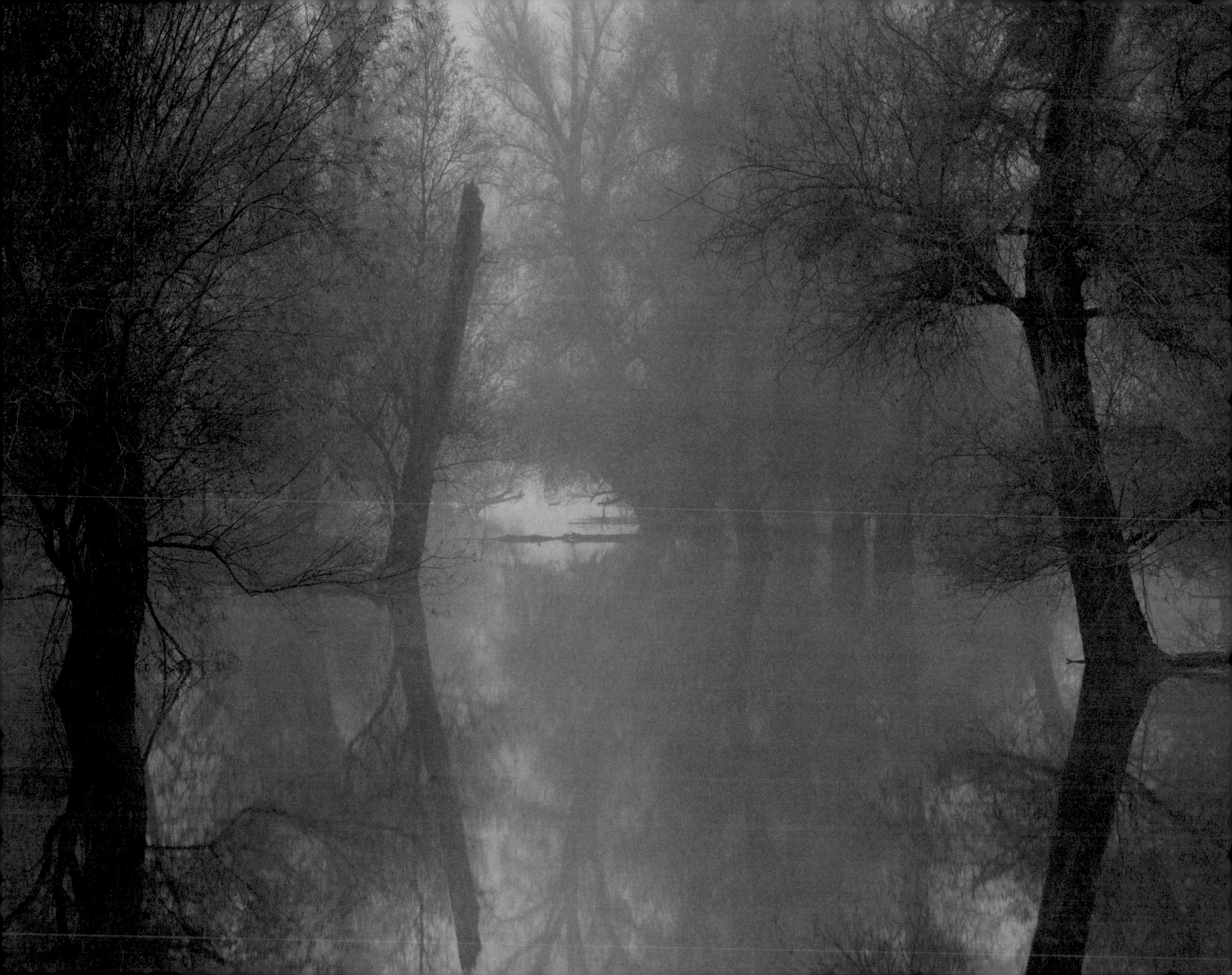

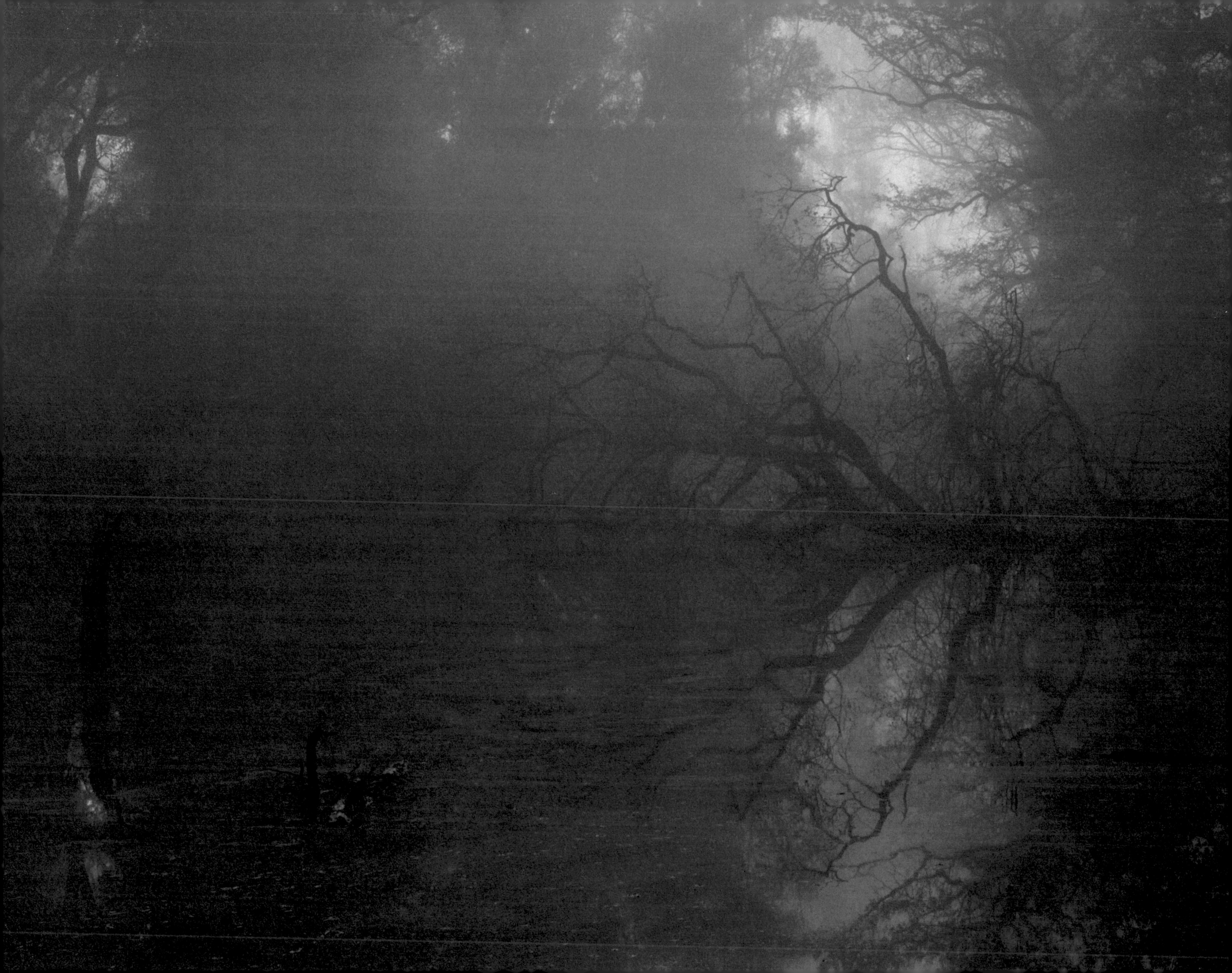

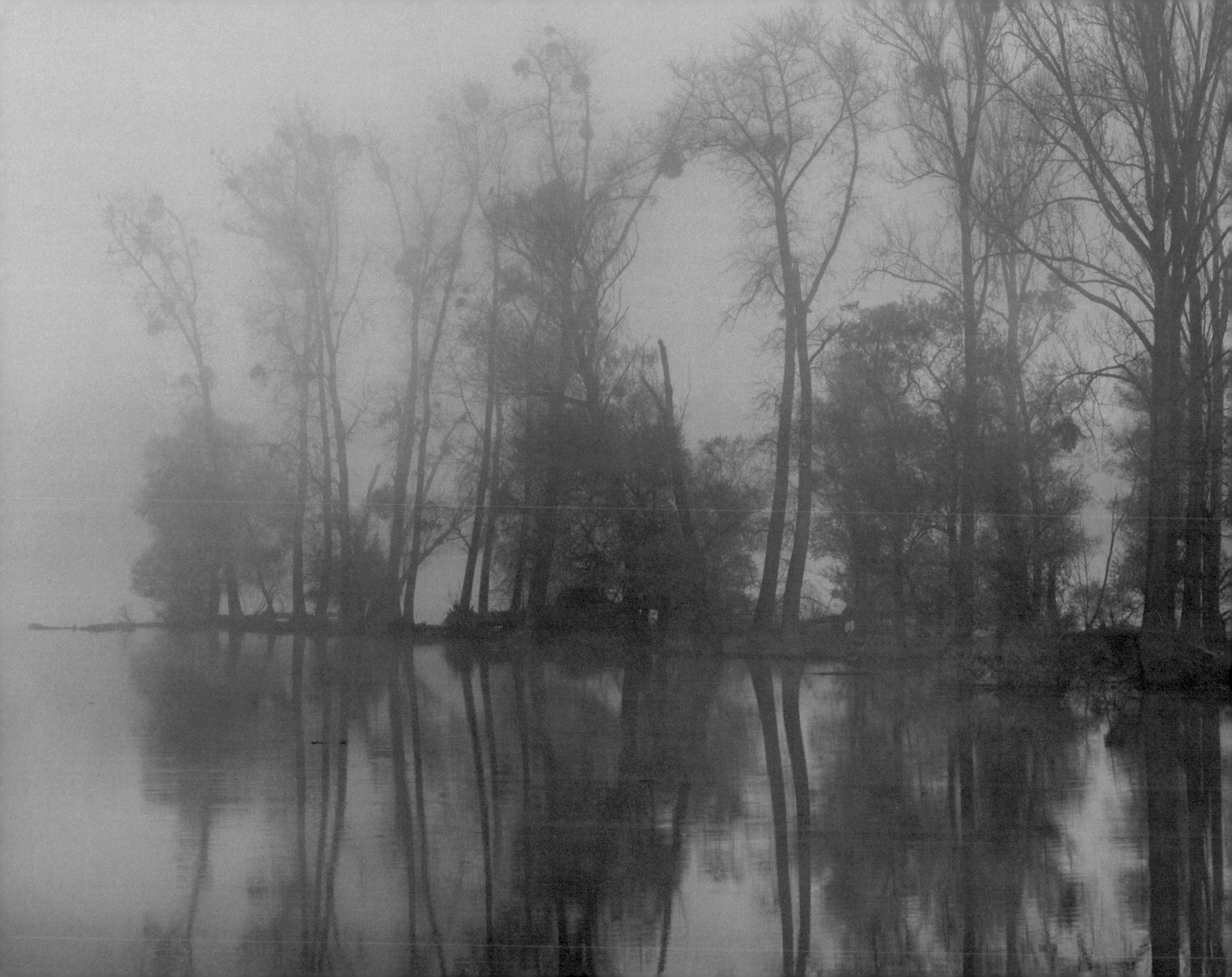

R 3498

R 2595

R 7808

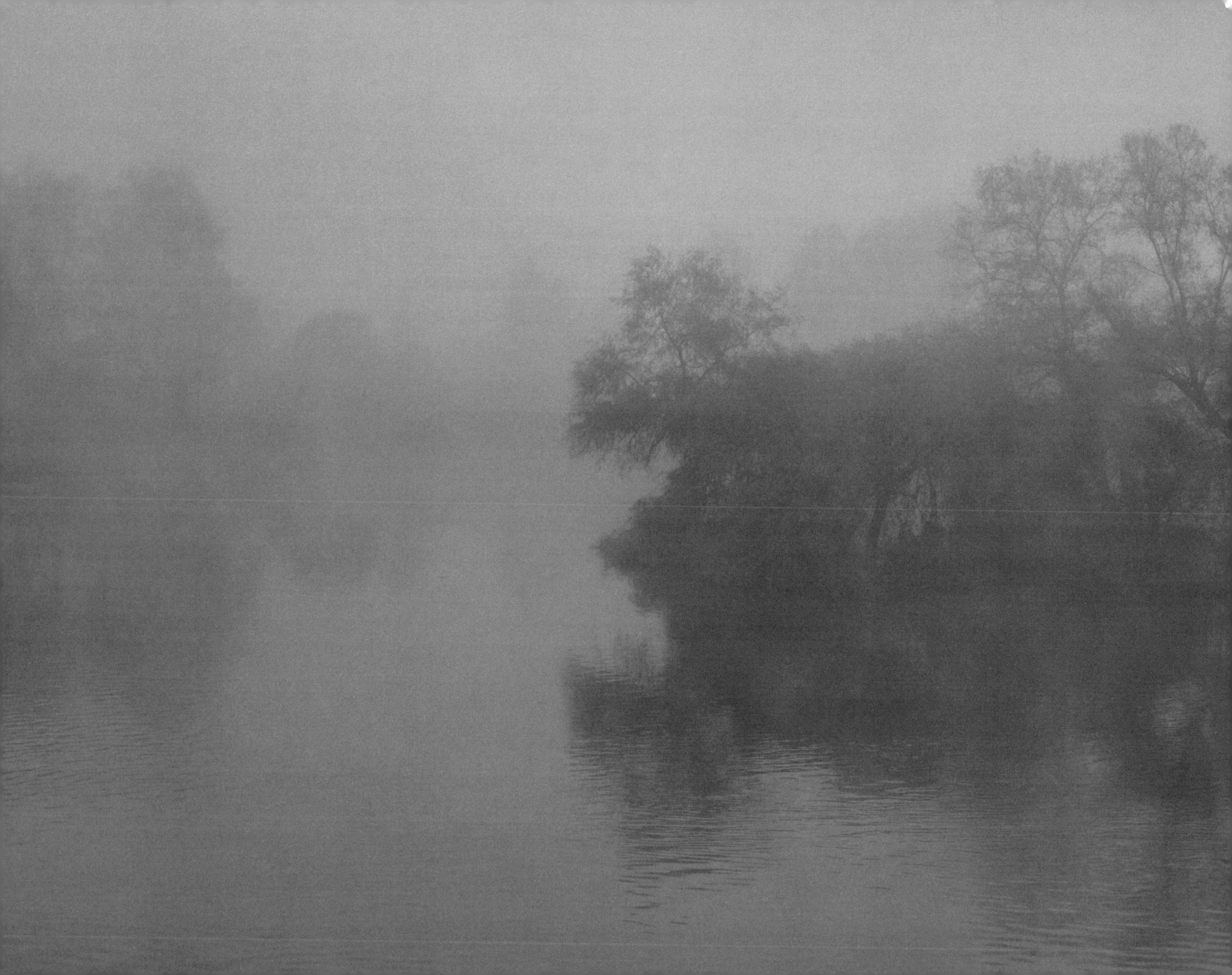

If a straight line

If the note of a birdsong filled air from the tree to the sky
in a straight line, we could follow the song

and hear silence on one side, and music on the other,
and the clarity of a clear sound like clear water

would orient through to the other side of everything
that ever mattered, that ever could, sonically illuminating

what we are supposed to have figured out by now.

But of course, a birdcall uncoils and releases itself
across air like fog through trees, forcing forgiveness

of the windstream for pushing notes and nuance
in every direction, while the river below,

flowing under the sound, courses forward, ever forward,
the fluency of gravity and determination of current

to move around and over and despite rocks, fallen branches.

It is not terra firma wisdom, this easy and inevitable flow,
this kind of trust, and neither is music from birds, for that matter.

Or the winter light splaying the gray long days, or prayer
or memory. Yet here I stand on the banks of this river,

needing every single thing I cannot see and do not understand,
watching the water and shadows of trees synchronously

move together, carrying everything in their path toward somewhere.

And where does happiness fit into all this—what's the sound
of hope and belief and of finally just letting go?

And where the river melts into some ocean
is that the inevitable blending of intention and outcome,

rimmed by a never-shifting horizon line splitting sky and earth?
Or, rather, wrapping around like string or arms

holding the world, its sounds, our mistakes, the proof together.

KIRSTEN RIAN

Einer geraden Linie gleich

Zöge sich der Gesang der Vögel von den Bäumen bis zum Himmel
in einer geraden Linie, so könnten wir dem Lied folgen

und Stille auf der einen und Musik auf der andren Seite vernehmen,
und die Klarheit eines klaren Klangs würde klarem Wasser gleich

sich richten hin zur andren Seite aller Dinge,
die jemals zählten, die jemals klanglich erhellten,

was wir längst sollten erkannt haben.

Hingegen, der Ruf eines Vogels löst sich schwebend
durch die Luft wie Nebel durch die Bäume, Vergebung verlangend

vom Strom des Windes, der Klänge und Nuancen
in alle Richtungen zerstreut, während der Fluss darunter

unter dem Schall quellend schnellt, vorwärts, immer vorwärts
das Geschmeidige der Schwerkraft, das Entschlossene der Strömung

zu treiben, um und über und trotz Felsen, gefallenem Geäst.

Er birgt keine verlässliche Weisheit, dieser leichte, unabänderliche Fluss,
diese Art von Zuversicht und auch nicht die Musik der Vögel

oder das Licht des Winters, das die grauen langen Tage dehnt, das Gebet
nicht oder die Erinnerung. Und doch stehe ich hier am Ufer dieses Stroms,

brauche jedes kleine Ding, das ich nicht sehen kann und nicht verstehn,
schaue auf das Wasser und die Schatten jener Bäume, wie sie

zueinander streben, ein jedes auf ihrem Weg tragend, irgendwohin.

Und wo passt das Glück in all dies hinein – wie ist der Klang
von Hoffnung, Glaube und letzlichem Loslassen?

Und wo der Fluss mit einem Meer verschmilzt,
ist es dort, wo sich Absicht und Wirkung auf immer vermengen,

gerahmt von einem geraden, festen Horizont, der Himmel und Erde trennt?
Oder, mehr noch, umschlingend als wären es Kordeln oder Arme,

verbindend die Welt, ihre Klänge, unsere Fehler und das Wissen darum.

KIRSTEN RIAN

R 2569

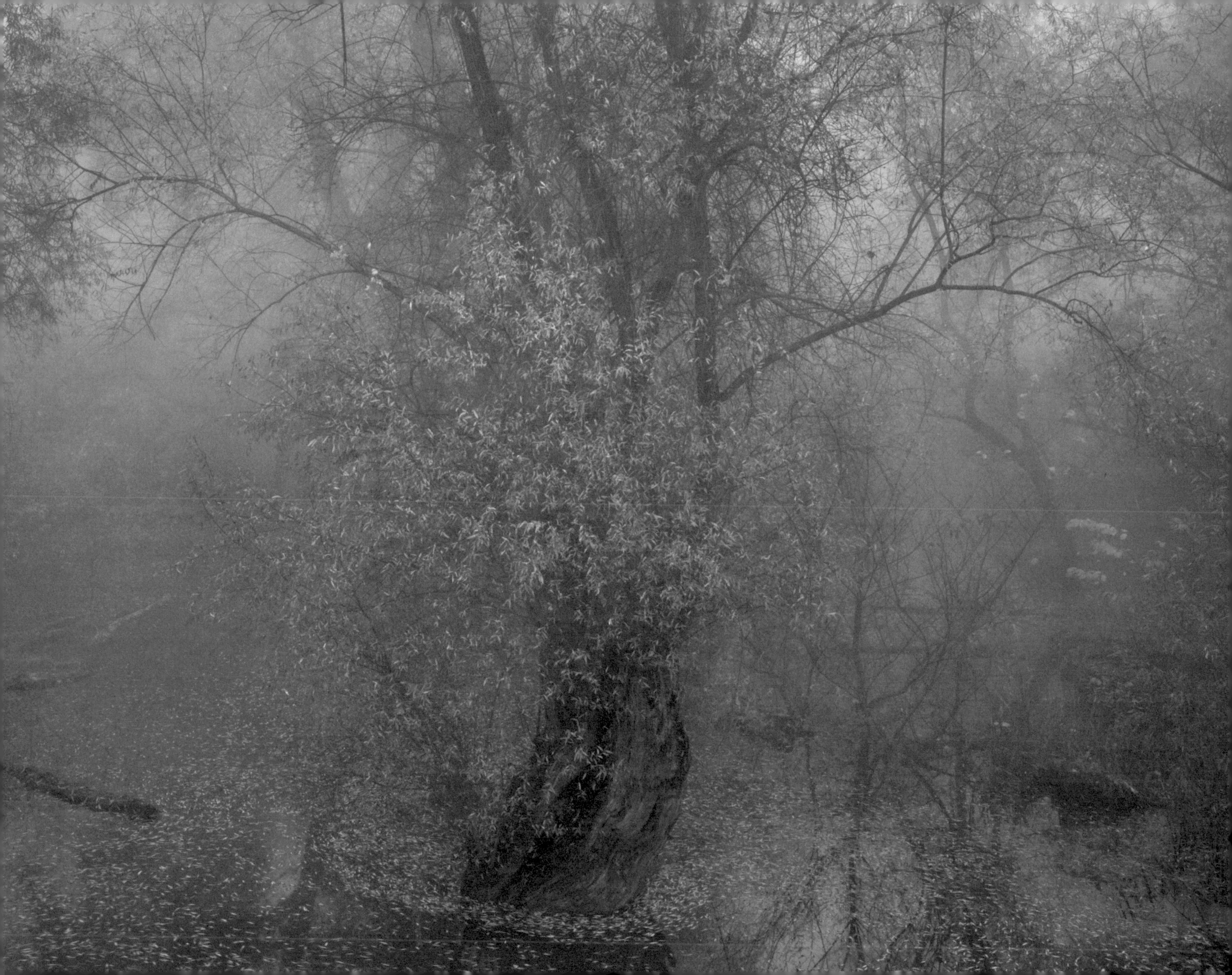

R 7763

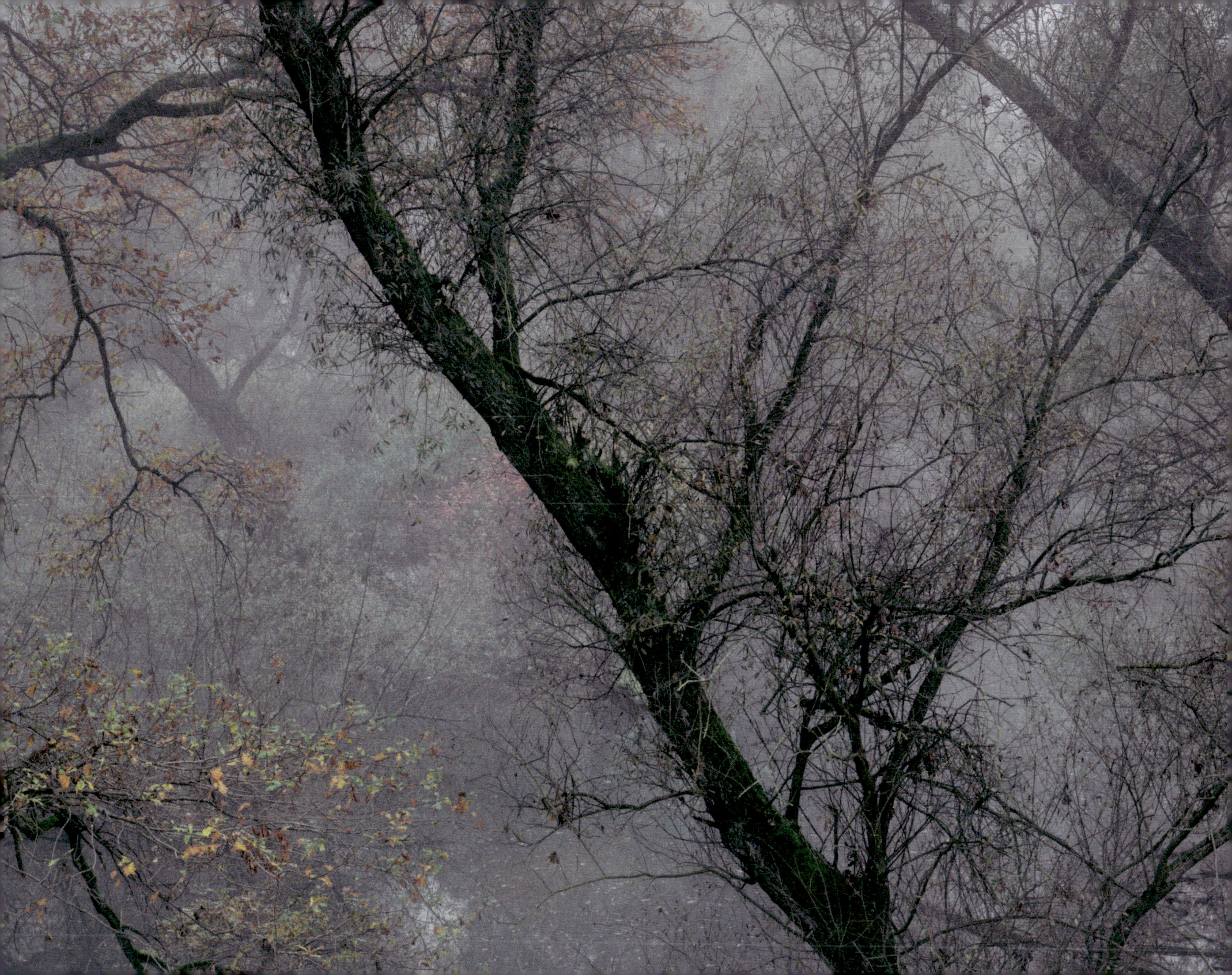

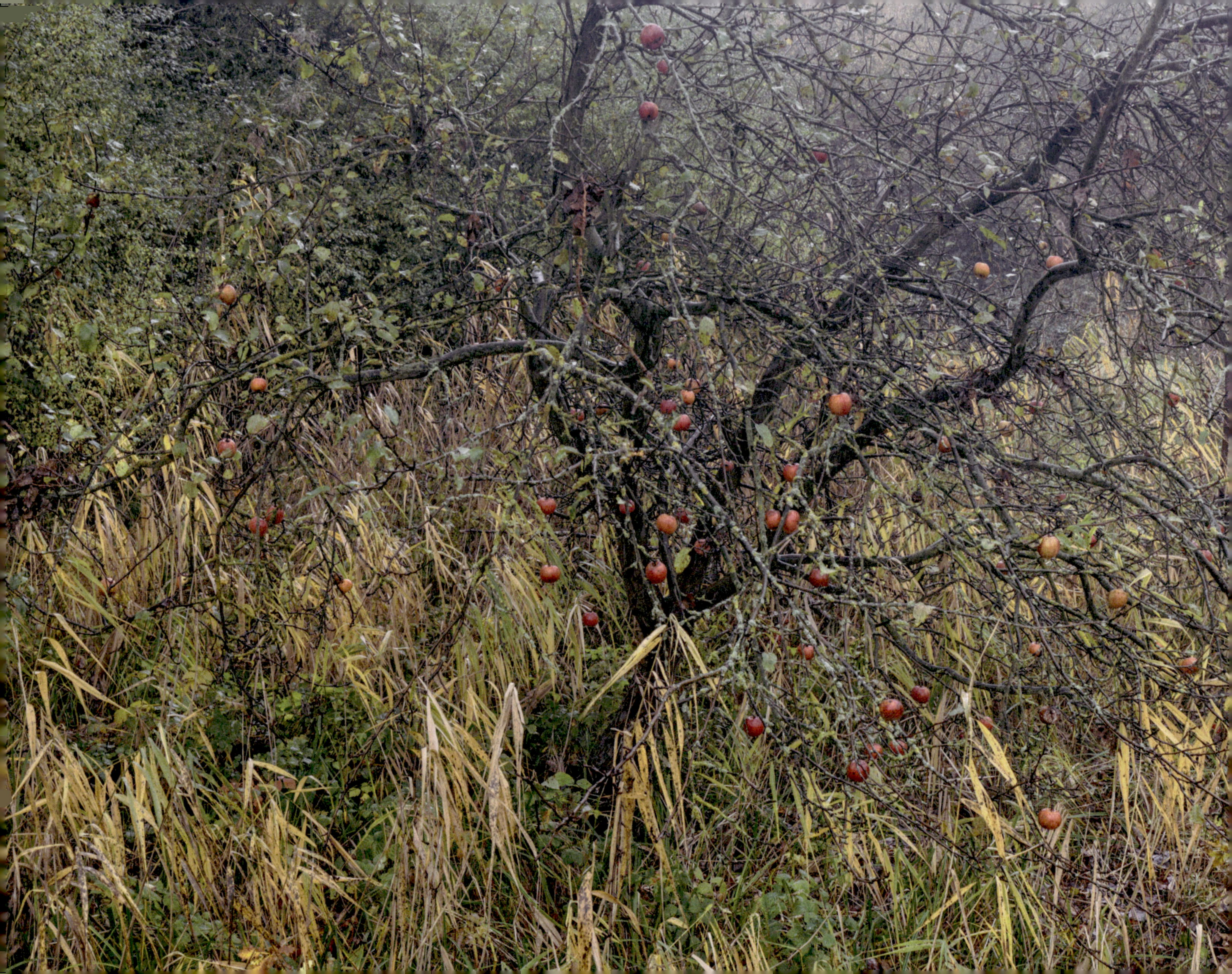

R 8270

Two limited **COLLECTOR'S EDITIONS**, original works of art by Michael Lange, are available with this book:
Zu diesem Buch sind zwei limitierte Originalarbeiten von Michael Lange als COLLECTOR'S EDITION erhältlich:

Michael Lange
R 8953, 2014
R 0825, 2012

Two inkjet prints on Hahnemühle paper, in folder, with book
Sheet size: 42.6 × 33 cm, image size: 38.6 × 29 cm
Limited edition of 12 + 5 a. p. each, signed and numbered
€ 580.00 per motif, set € 1,060.00 *
Zwei Inkjet-Prints auf Hahnemühle-Papier, in Mappe, mit Buch
Blattformat: 42,6 × 33 cm, Bildformat: 38,6 × 29 cm
Auflage: je 12 + 5 a. p., signiert und nummeriert
Je Motiv € 580,–, Set € 1 060,– *

For more information or to place an order, please contact Hatje Cantz at *ce@hatjecantz.de*, or visit our website, www.hatjecantz.com.
Mit weiteren Fragen oder Ihrer Bestellung wenden Sie sich bitte an *ce@hatjecantz.de* oder besuchen Sie unsere Internetseite www.hatjecantz.de.

* **Price as of March 2015, subject to change**
* Stand 3/2015, Preisänderungen vorbehalten

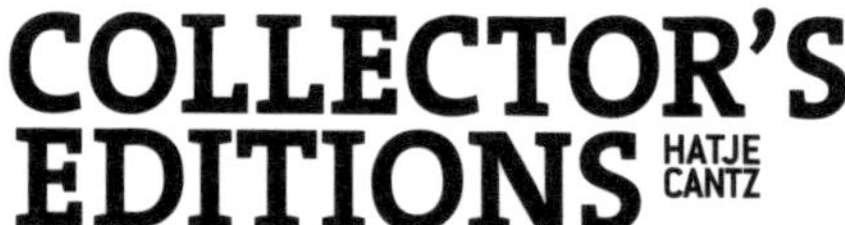

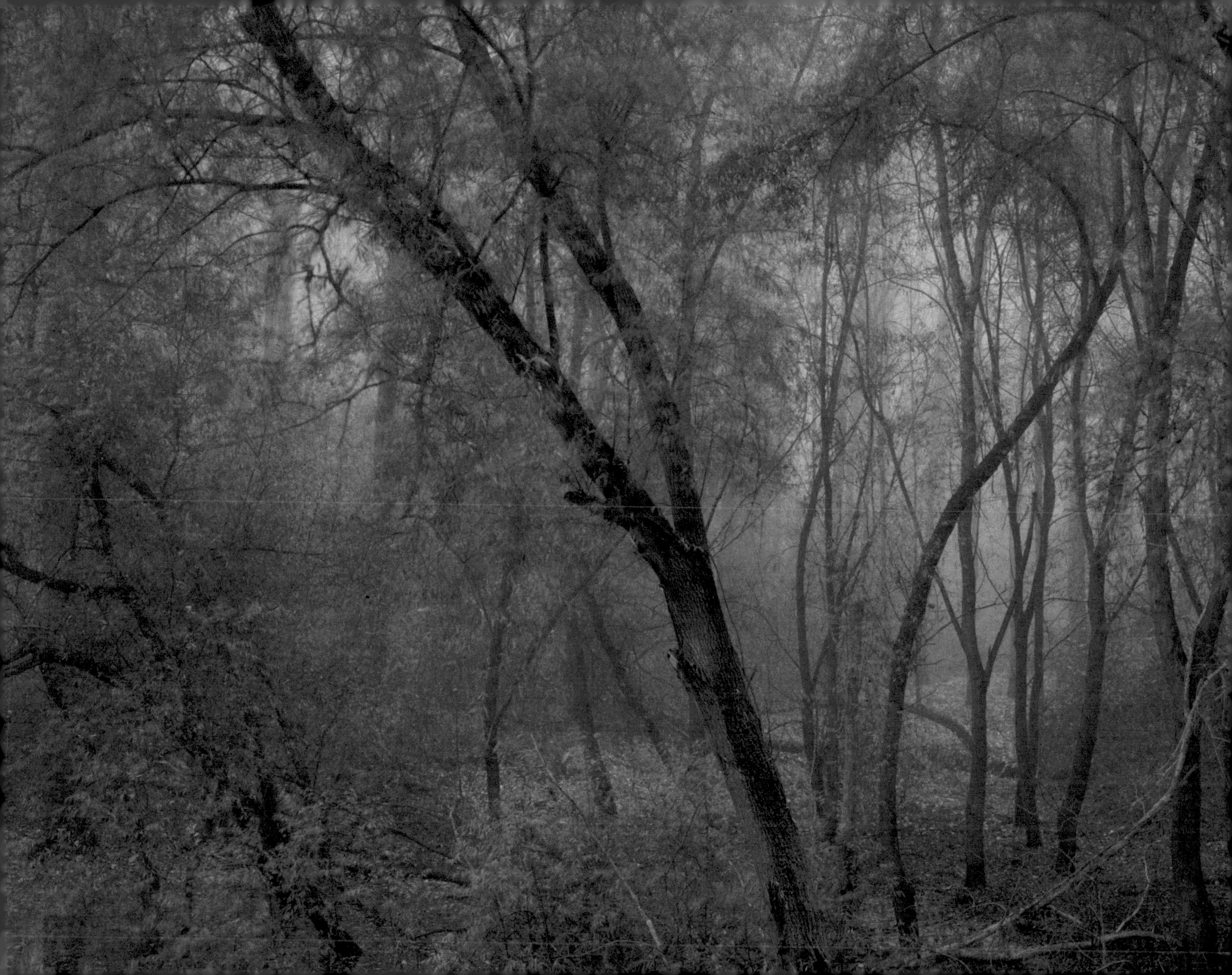

R 2004

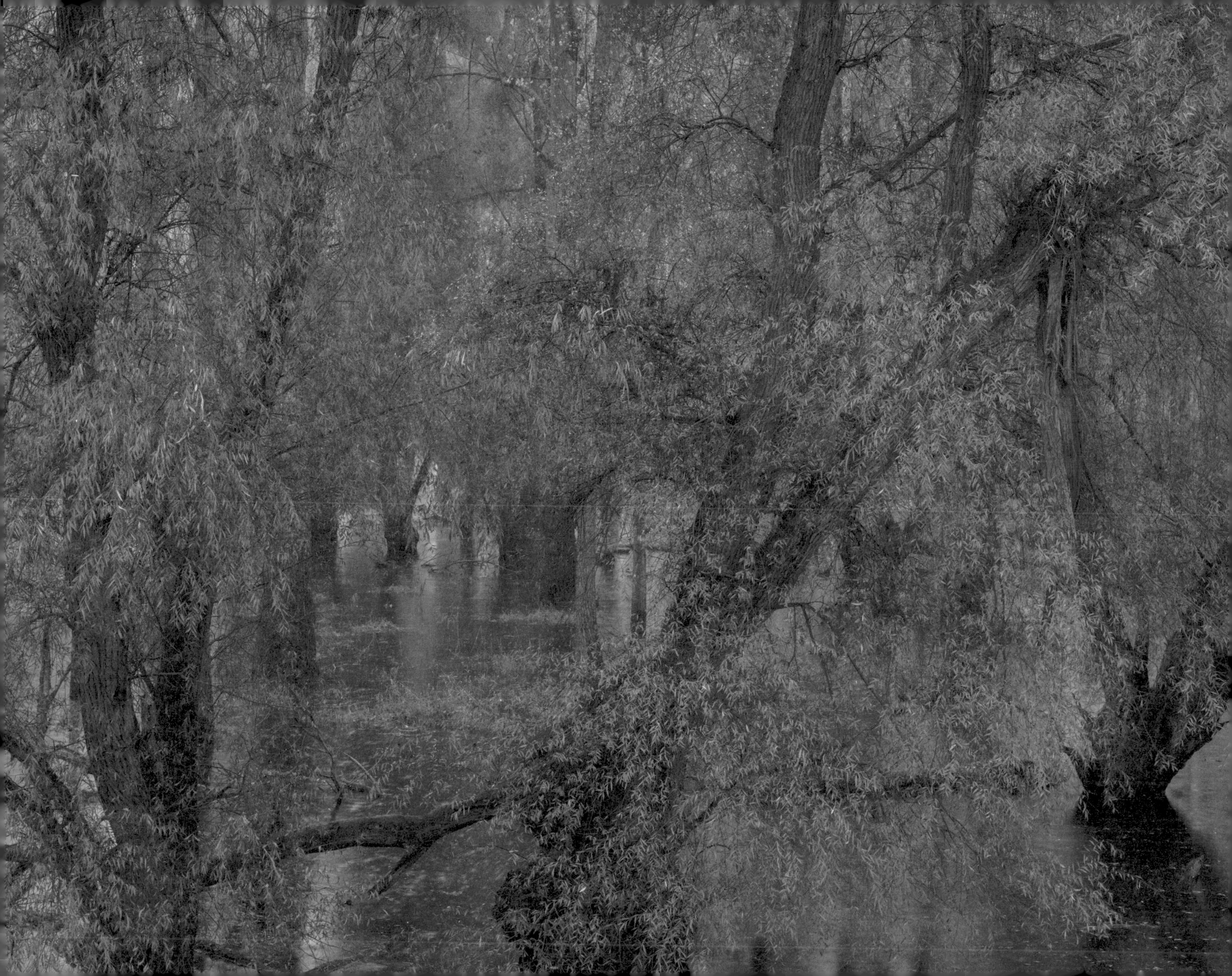

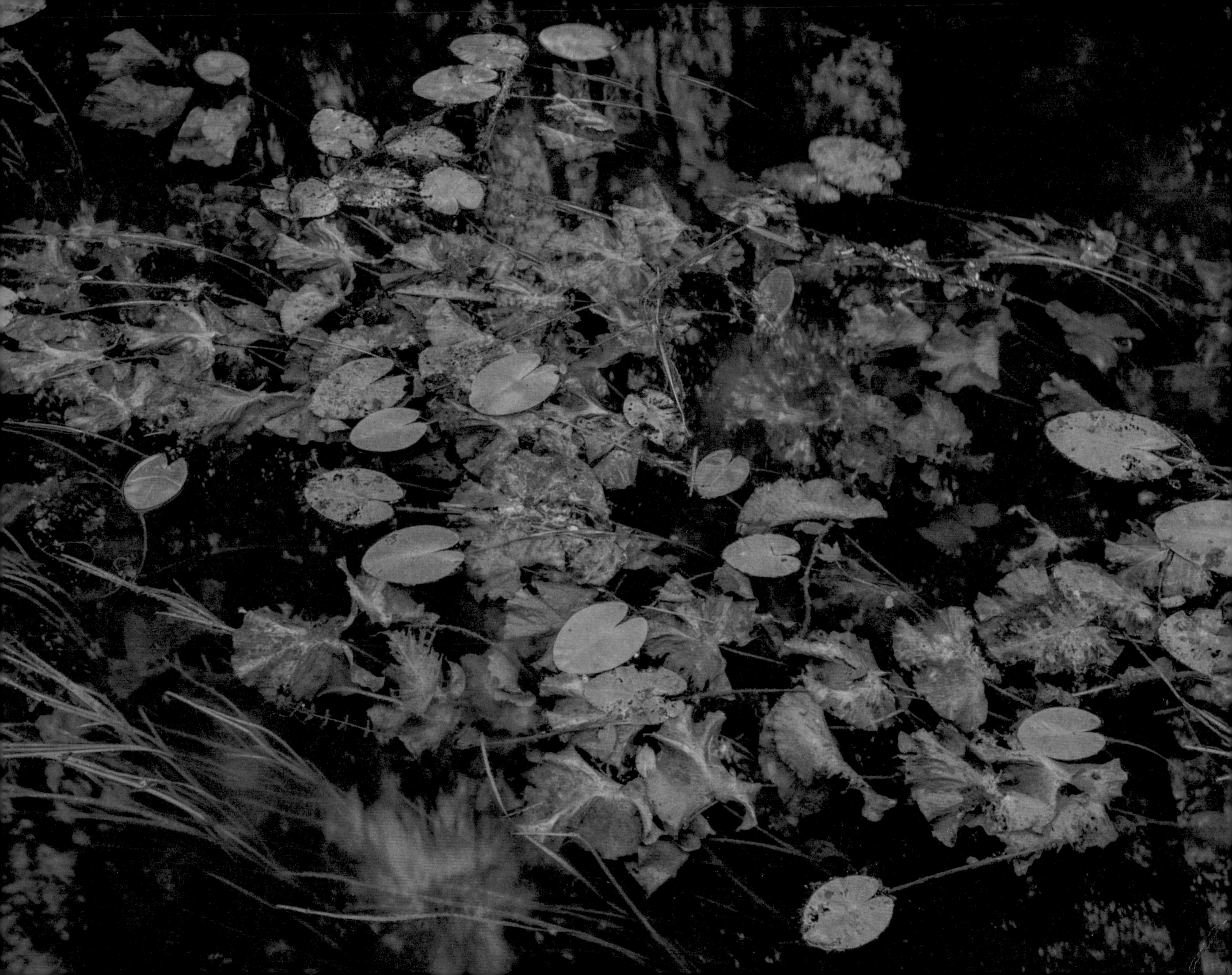

R 0760

R 4085

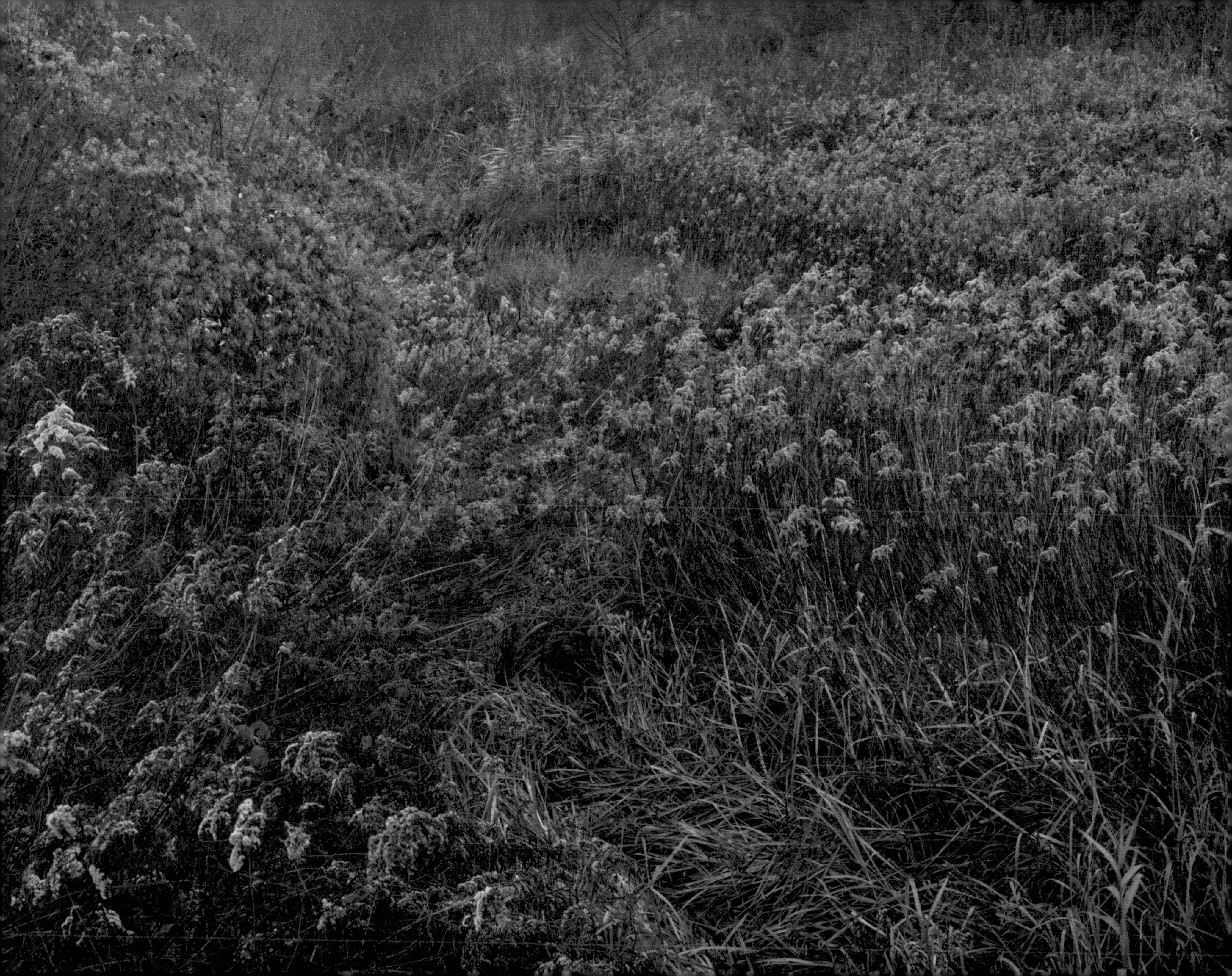

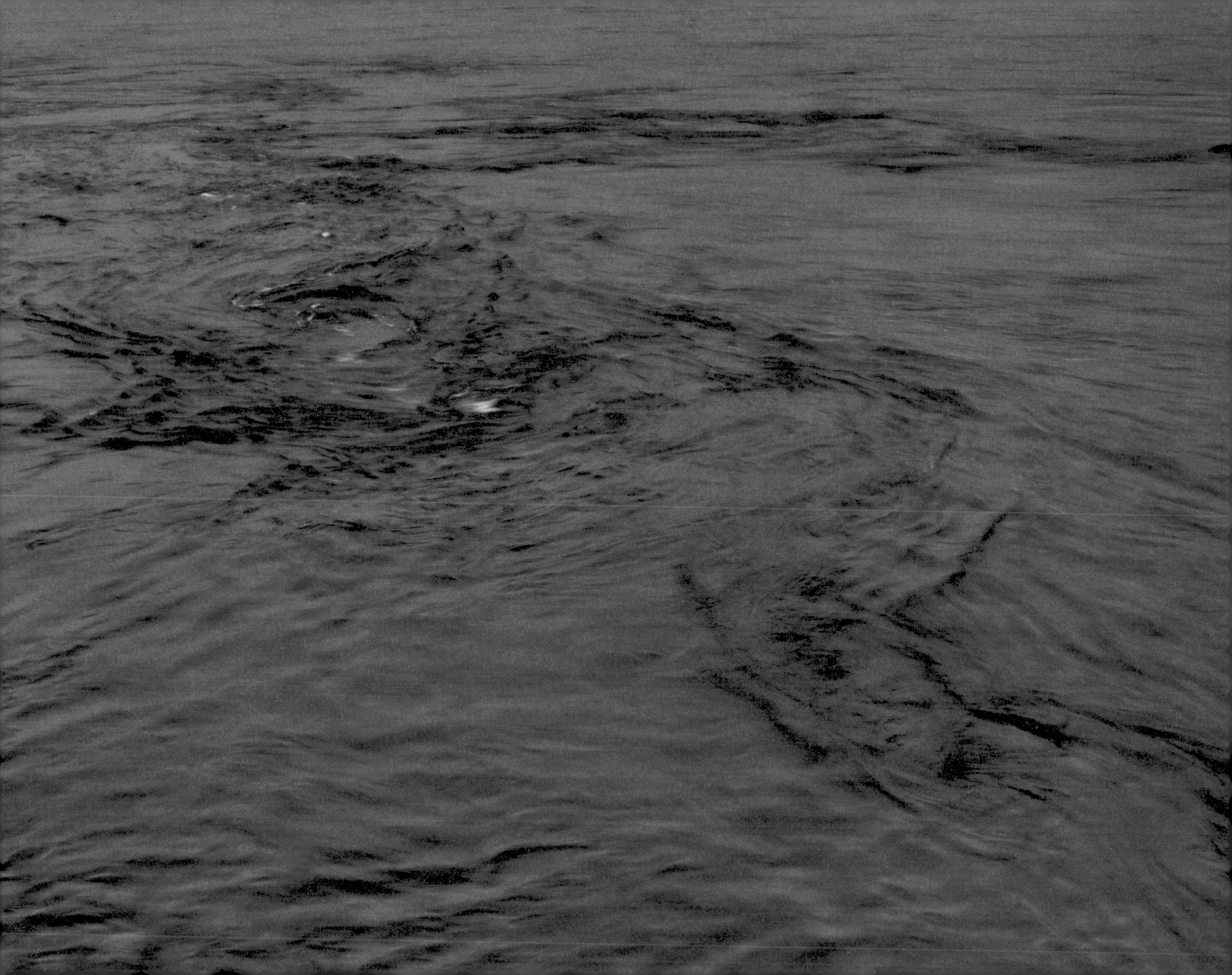

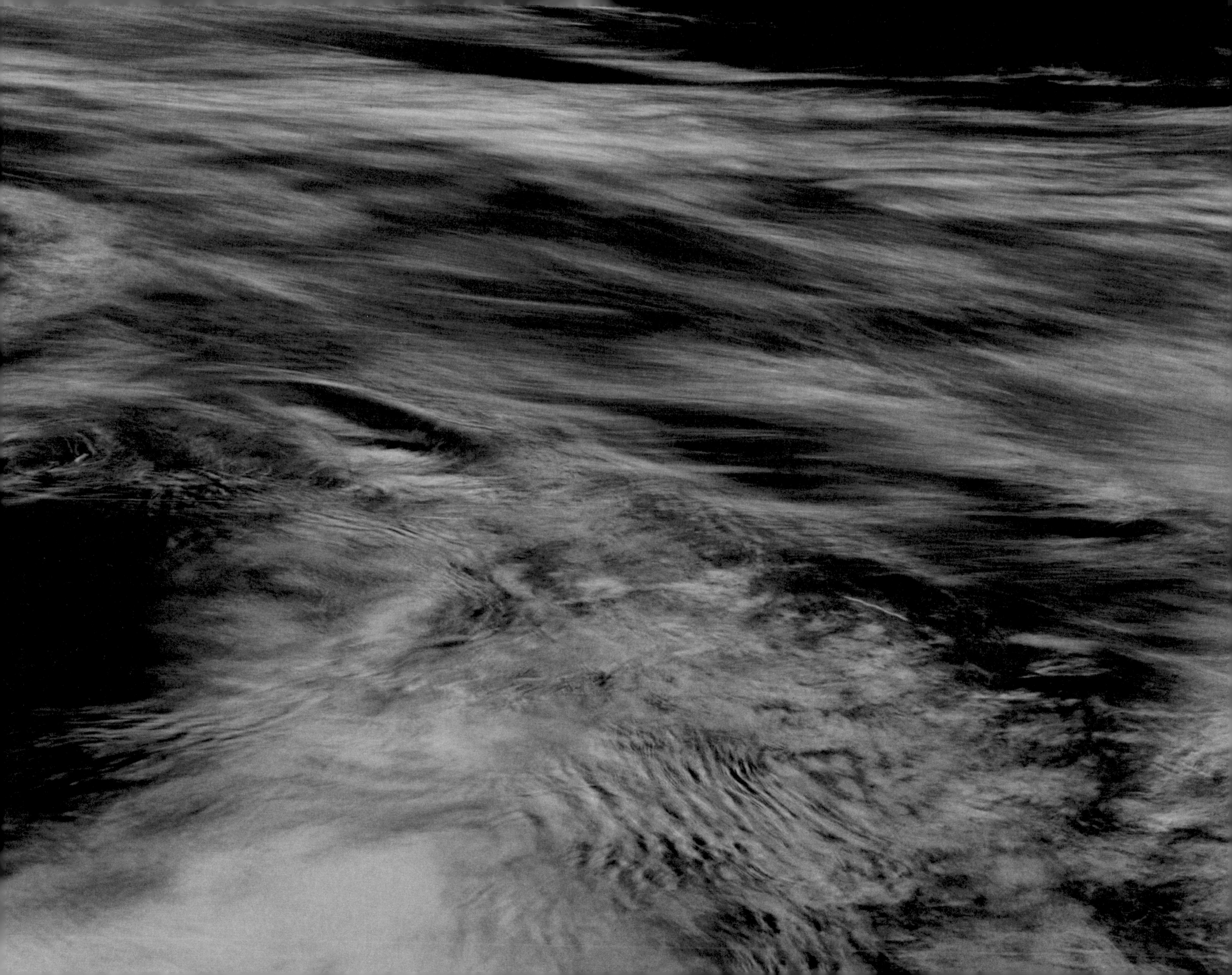

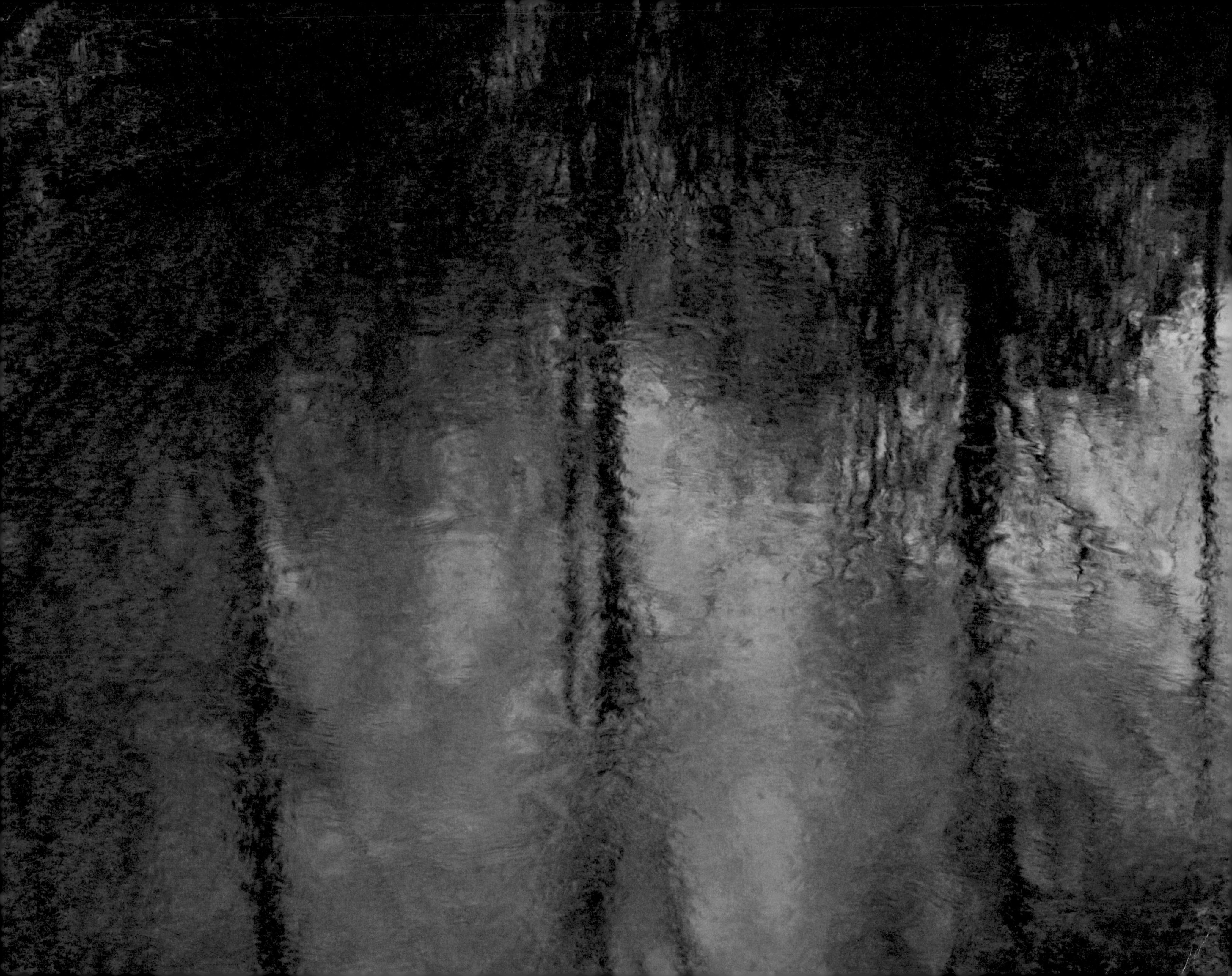

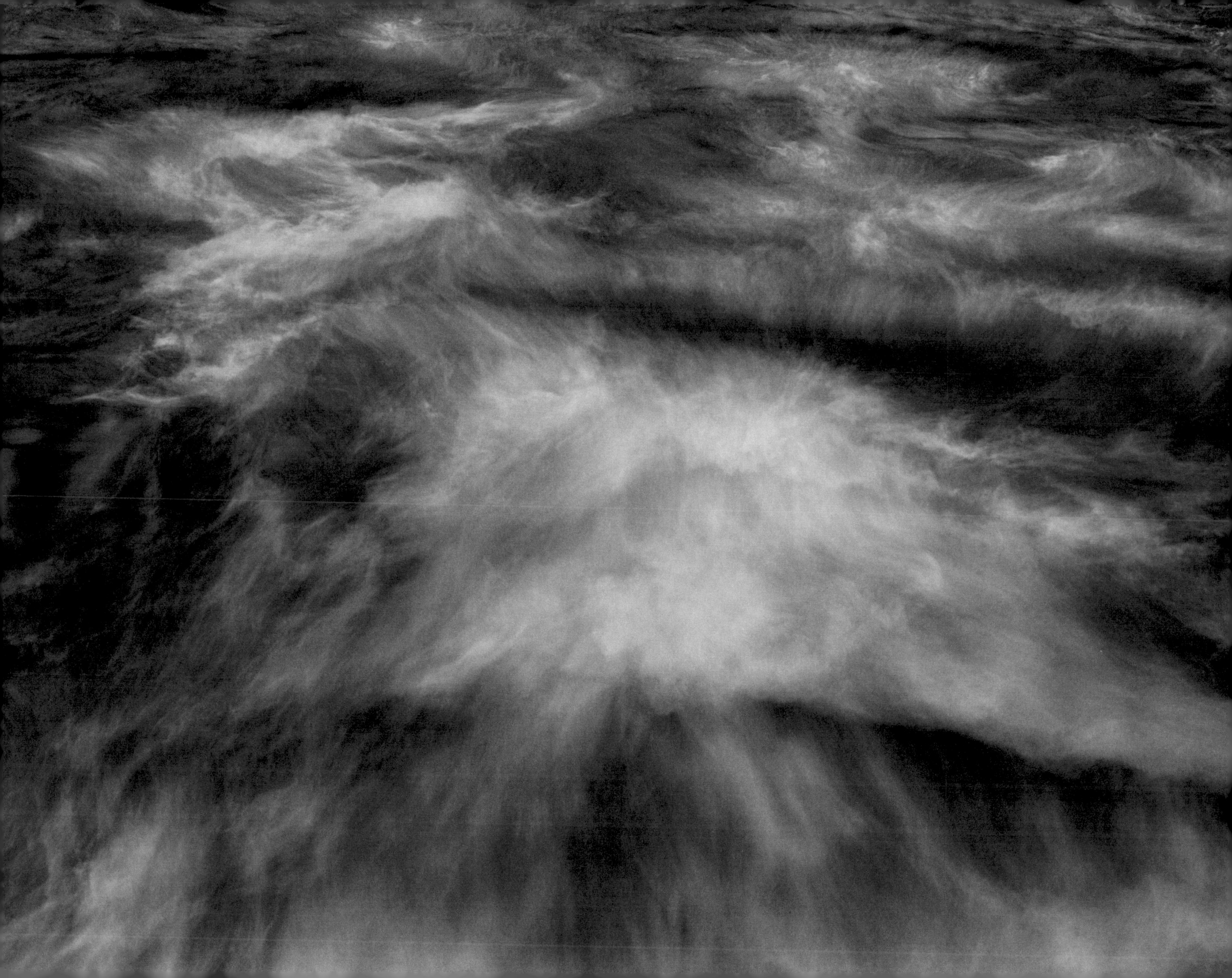

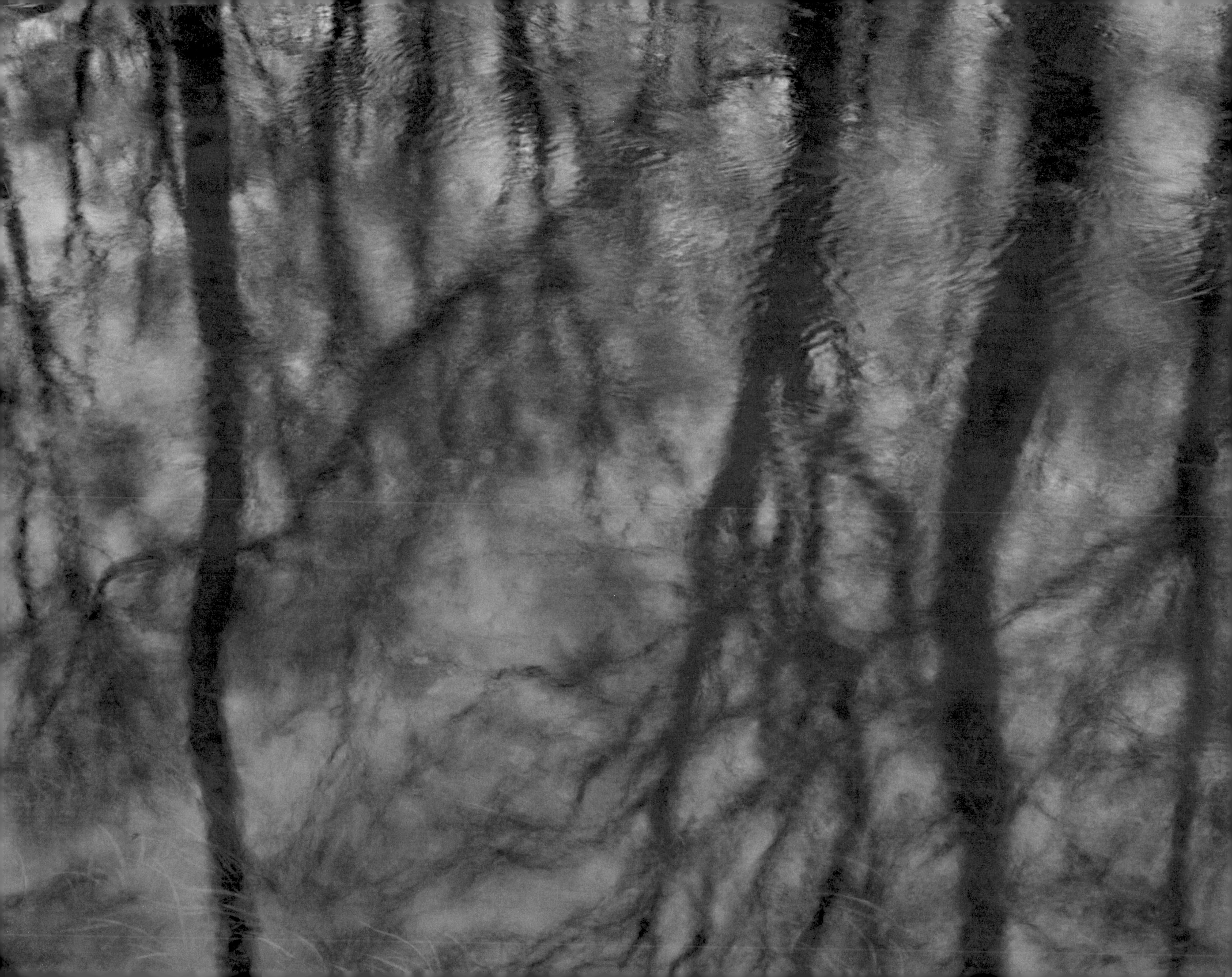

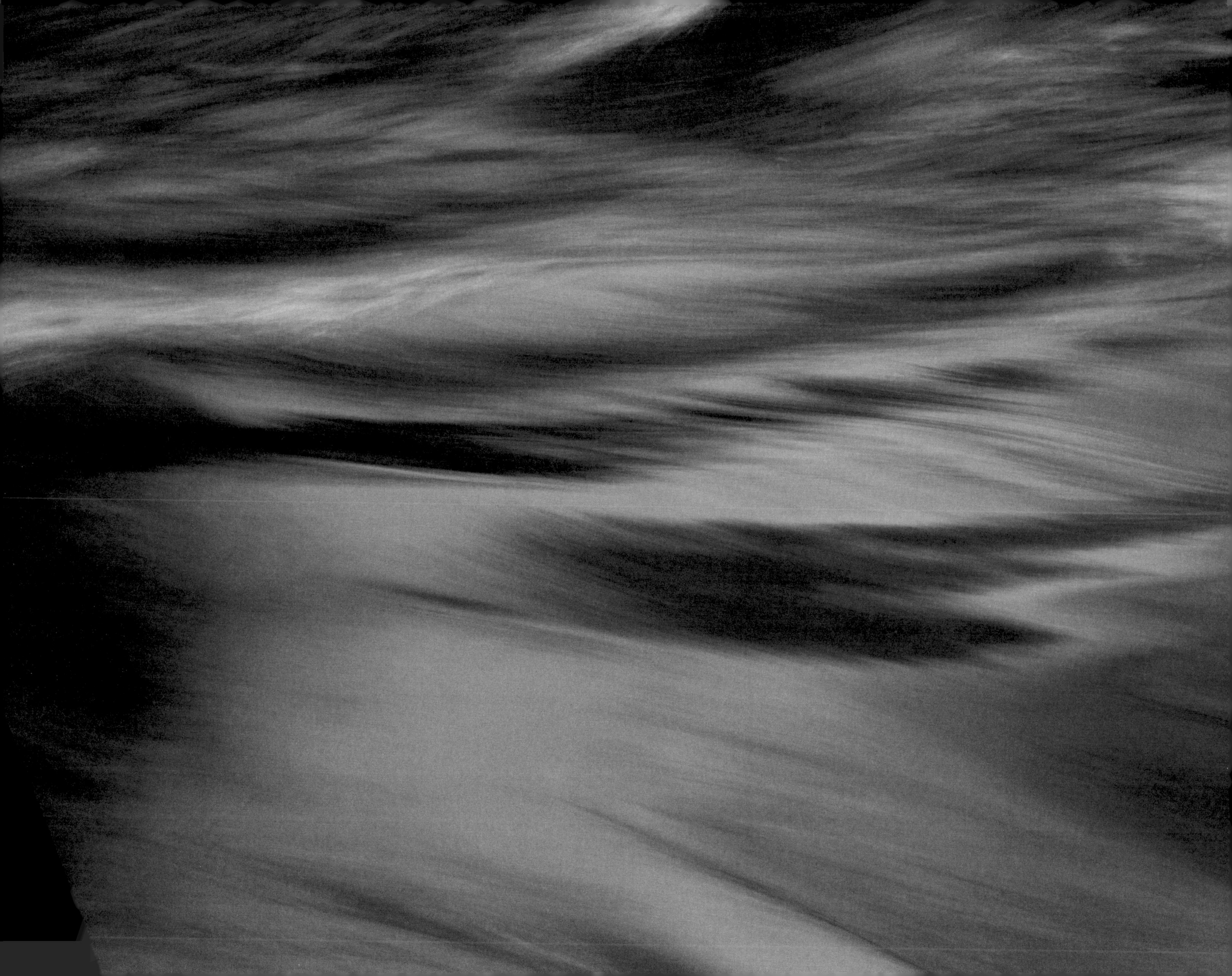

R 9902

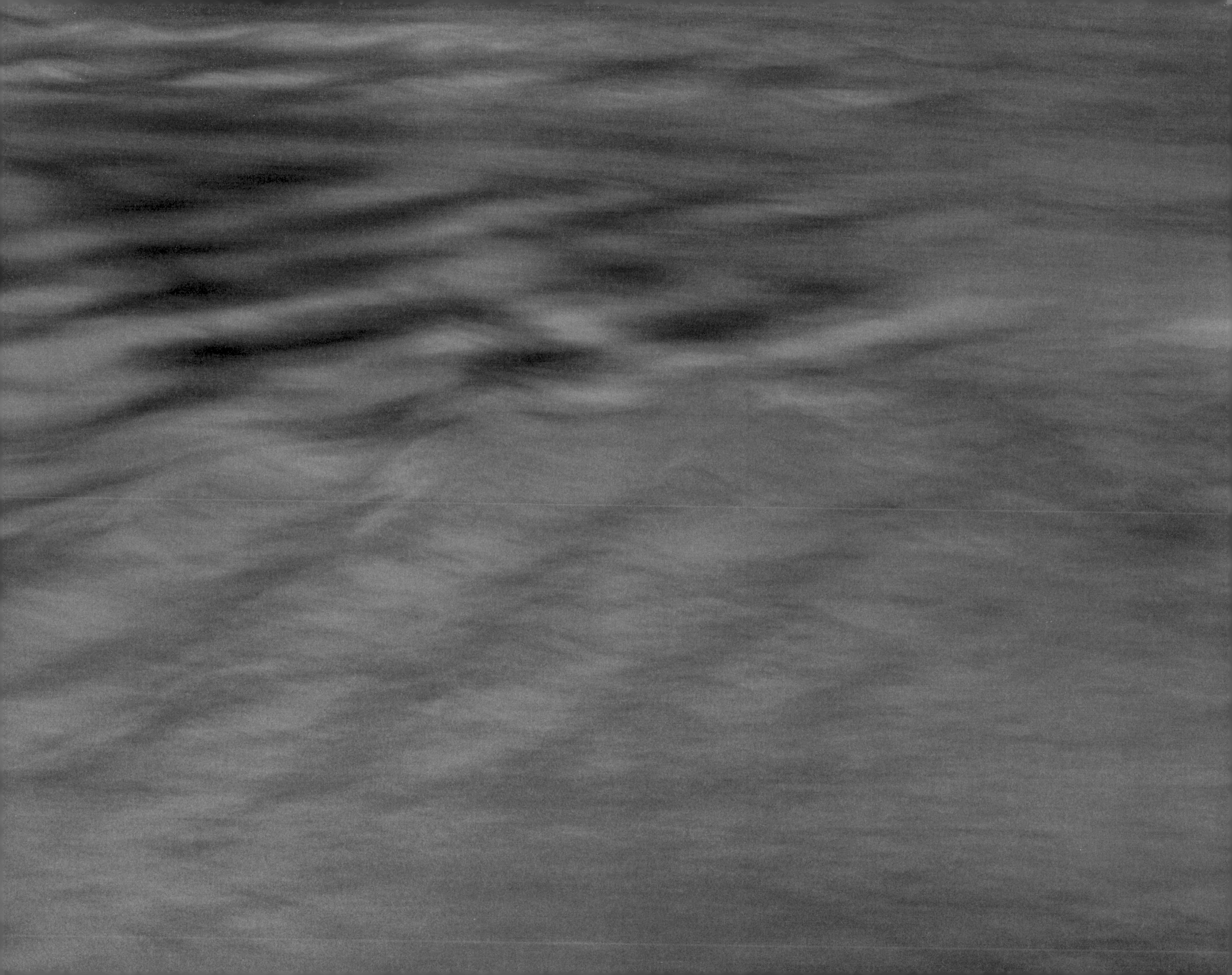

MICHAEL LANGE – *fluss*

Editor Herausgeber: Nadine Barth, Hatje Cantz
Copyediting Lektorat: Leina González
Translation Übersetzung: Nadine Barth (Poem Gedicht), Alexandra Titze-Grabec
Graphic design Grafische Gestaltung: Anke Rabba
Typefaces Schriften: TheSans, Linotype Univers, TheMix
Fine drawing Reinzeichnung: Markus Schaefer, take shape media design
Reproductions Reproduktionen: Jan Scheffler, prints professional
Production Herstellung: Nadine Schmidt, Hatje Cantz
Paper Papier: GardaPat Kiara, 150 g/m²
Printing and binding Gesamtherstellung: DZA Druckerei zu Altenburg GmbH

Thank You! Dankeschön!
Anke Rabba, Beate Mangler, Christiane Stahl, Claudia Willke, Claudia Barlett, Colin Turner, Emy Koen, Gerd Ludwig, Hans von Hirsch, Harf Zimmermann, Kisten Rian, Lothar Albrecht, Joseph Bellows, Milena Schäufele, Nadine Schmidt, Rixon Reed, Robert Morat, Stephen Cohen, and especially und besonders Nadine Barth.

With the generous support of the Mit großzügiger Unterstützung der
ALFRED EHRHARDT STIFTUNG

Further thanks to the Forest Administration of Rhineland-Palatinate and the Ministry of Rural Affairs and Consumer Protection of Baden-Wuerttemberg for the friendly endorsements.
Dankeschön auch an das Ministerium für Ländlichen Raum und Verbraucherschutz in Baden-Württemberg, sowie an die Landesforsten von Rheinland-Pfalz für die freundlichen Genehmigungen.

Published in Erschienen im
Hatje Cantz Verlag
Zeppelinstrasse 32
73760 Ostfildern
Germany Deutschland
Tel. +49 711 4405-200, Fax -220
www.hatjecantz.com
A Ganske Publishing Group company

Hatje Cantz books are available internationally at selected bookstores. For more information about our distribution partners, please visit our website at www.hatjecantz.com.

ISBN 978-3-7757-3962-7
Printed in Germany

fluss was photographed between 2012 and 2014 along the Upper Rhine in Southern Germany. It is Michael Lange's second book.
fluss entstand in den Jahren zwischen 2012 und 2014 entlang des Oberrheins in Süddeutschland. Es ist Michael Langes zweites Buch.

This book will be acompanied by a series of exhibitions internationally. Further informations at www.michaellange.eu

Two limited COLLECTOR'S EDITIONS are available with this book: *R 0825,* 2012; *R 8953,* 2014. For more information, please contact Hatje Cantz at ce@hatjecantz.de.

Diese Publikation wird von einer internationalen Ausstellungsreihe begleitet. Weitere Informationen unter www.michaellange.eu

Zu diesem Buch sind zwei limitierte Originalarbeiten als COLLECTOR'S EDITION erhältlich: *R 0825,* 2012; *R 8953,* 2014. Mit weiteren Fragen wenden Sie sich bitte an ce@hatjecantz.de.